INTRODUCTION

PICTURESQUE CHESHIRE was published in 1903 and paints a glowing picture of the Cheshire countryside in the closing years of the nineteenth century. T.A. Coward, who wrote several books about Cheshire's history, topography and natural history, writes about its towns, villages and countryside with great knowledge and enthusiasm. Some of his descriptions will be familiar to readers even after almost a century, others will be less so—quiet country lanes are now busy highways swamped by twentieth century traffic; many green fields and woodlands have been swallowed up by spreading towns and numerous old buildings have either fallen down or been removed to make way for new developments.

This is particularly true of Wirral where the success of the Port of Liverpool during the late eighteenth and nineteenth centuries resulted in a great surge of residential and industrial development along the Mersey which has continued to the present time.

In his text T.A. Coward laments the relentless urbanisation of Birkenhead, but I wonder what he would make of Wirral today. Much has changed—Poole Hall, which he says is "perhaps the finest of the old Wirral halls" now lies under the factories which lie between the M53 and the Mersey, while the "villages" of Bebington, Bromborough and Eastham have become large sprawling towns. Ellesmere Port was little more than a handful of buildings at the terminus of the Shropshire Union Canal in 1903 while Whitby, Great

Sutton and Stanney were the smallest of villages surrounded by farmland.

Even the rural west has changed. Heswall is no longer a small village surrounded by rolling heathland, but one of the main settlements on this side of Wirral. But perhaps the change which has had the greatest effect of all in the west is the loss of the Dee Estuary. A hundred years ago siltation of the river was well advanced and reclamation schemes had been taking place for over two centuries; but compare his view of Parkgate and Neston with that of today; or the outlook from Burton Point across what was then tidal flats which reached almost to Shotwick Church.

This little book has been created from two chapters from *"Picturesque Cheshire"* and has been reproduced here as faithfully as possible. None of the spelling has been changed and the original illustrations, produced by Roger Oldham, have also been included.

Carl Rogers
1998

HALTON BOROUGH COUNCIL	
Cypher	13.12.02
	£2.50

CHAPTER 1

WESTERN WIRRAL

The waters of the Dee once washed the walls of Chester at the Water Tower; from here on a clear day the old river bank is plainly visible, Blacon Point, a steep headland, standing above the flat lands of Sealand. Verdant fields, far as the eye can reach, stretch away to the north and west—lands stolen from the sea, politically belonging to Flint, the artificial navigable "Cut" having been constructed far on the Welsh side of the old river bed. Blacon, the southern limit of the great Forest of Wirral, was more of a tree-grown forest than the other two Cheshire hunting domains.

> From Blacon Point to Hilbree
> Squirrels in search of food
> Might then jump straight from tree to tree,
> So thick the forest stood.

This is Leigh's version of the old quatrain. Formby Point is sometimes substituted for Blacon and cited as proof that the Mersey did not flow by its present channel, but joined the Dee south of Hilbre. Possibly the Mersey did not always flow in its present channel, but entered the sea between Wallasey and Meols. Wirral Forest, ruled by the Stanleys by right of the horn, was the earliest to be disforested. Leaving Chester by Northgate, I pass Bache Hall to the two Mollingtons, above the village of Great Saughall, where at the close of the seventeenth century lived Mary Davies.

You that love wonders to behold,
Here you may of a wonder read,
The strangest that was ever seen or told,
A woman with horns upon her head.

The unhealthy growths, termed horns, "sadly grieving the old woman, especially upon the change of weather," were the means of Mary's livelihood, for she exhibited herself "at the sign of the Swan near Charing Cross" to a wondering public. People of note visited her, and as at certain periods she shed her horns, they were purchased for museums and private collections. "One of them an English lord obtained and presented it to the French king," while others went to the Ashmolean and British Museum. Before she was thirty she began to grow horns, and for over forty years supported herself on the profits of excrescences.

Beyond Great Mollington is Gibbet Mill, a relic of days when malefactors swung in chains beside the ill-paved road; the Chester Parkgate coach was dragged through the mud by six horses. Either the Queen's Ferry road or the next turning leads to Shotwick by a lane between luxuriant hedges that drops towards the Dee. Shotwick is on the edge of the ancient tide-mark; not long ago barnacle geese could be shot from the shelter of the churchyard wall.

Shotwick Church has been restored but the tower is old. It has only one aisle, an old "three-decker" pulpit, and box pews; one at the west end, for the churchwardens, dated 1673, has a wooden canopy supported on turned oak pillars. A Norman doorway is screened by a timbered porch, yet this rough porch is so old that it would be a pity to lose it. When Saughall boomed its horned woman, Shotwick gained fame from the writings of its vicar—Dr. Samuel Clarke's *Martyrology*, a sort of revised "Fox."

The ancient residence of the Hockenhulls of Shotwick is gone; but the house erected by Joseph Hockenhull in 1662 remains, overgrown with ivy and creepers, snug within its walled garden. In the fifteenth century the Hockenhulls claimed all fish captured in the Dee where it touched their property, with the exception of whales, thirlsheads, and the royal sturgeons: these were the Earl's. The "Greyhound Inn" an inn no longer, was not built yesterday: note the great stone chimney, in strange contrast to the old red bricks. Shotwick Castle, one of the fortress guards for Chester, stood more than a mile up-stream; a mound and earthworks mark the site.

SHOTWICK CHURCH

A rough lane which led beneath the river bank exists no longer, but an uneven, grass-grown path by the Hall leads to Puddington. William Rufus gave the manor of Puddington to Hamo de Masci, "with bonds and limits from heaven above to hell beneath," and stipulated that Hamo was "to hold of me and mine with Bow and

Arrow when I shoot upon them," sealing the contract with his "wang tooth." William Massey, last lord of that name in possession of Puddington, fled from Preston after the rising of 1715. Fearing that the Mersey bridges would be watched, he swam his horse across the wide estuary to Hooton, and urged the jaded beast home across Wirral. It fell dead at its stable door. Massey tried the same ruse as Dick Turpin, for when near home he thrashed an unoffending countryman, who of course summoned him for assault. When arrested later he brought up this summons to prove an alibi; but the countryman got revenge, for Massey was frozen to death in Chester Castle.

Puddington Old Hall is much altered, but some of its timber and inside walls, and a great chimney-stack from the kitchen, date back many hundred years. John Pleasington, the family priest, hid in a secret chamber in this chimney, but was captured, and suffered at Chester for alleged sedition in 1679. The later Masseys, adhering to the Catholic faith, had a sorry time. In the wall which surrounds the remains of the moat are several heraldic stones, rescued from the fire when the New Hall was burnt many years ago.

Of all Deeside villages Burton is perhaps the most attractive, with its white thatched cottages and worn sandstone bed-rock footway along the single street. The Bishop of Lichfield and Coventry owned Burton, and under ecclesiastical law his tenants were allowed to keep dogs uncrippled by the "dog-guage." Elsewhere within the Forest all dogs had to pass their fore-feet through a small guage or ring, only one inch and a half by an inch in size, and if too large the unfortunate animal's feet were whittled down until they would go through. Little fear of the poor lamed creatures hunting the lord's deer or hares. Save at Burton sheepdogs could not be much use in Wirral.

Burton for more than a century belonged to the Congreves of Congreve and Stretton. William Congreve, poet and dramatist, lies in Westminster Abbey, through the influence of the Duchess of Marlborough, his more than patroness. He was brilliant, but his plays are coarse; he left his fortune to the Duchess, though Young the poet and others thought Mrs. Bracegirdle, the heroine of his plays, jilted for the more influential Duchess, deserved it. The Duchess, whose portrait, alongside that of the dramatist, hung in Burton Hall, squandered this money on a diamond necklace, an ivory clockwork

BURTON

figure, and a wax effigy of her late favourite, whose feet the silly woman wrapped in bandages as she wrapped those of the gouty Congreve.

Congreve of Stretton supported Charles II, and was to have been a knight of the Royal Oak. The institution of this order was dropped, but congreve received a picture of Mistress Jane Lane, the lady who, by pretending the king was her servant, effected his escape after that uncomfortable day at Boscobel. General Sir William Congreve invented a war rocket and Major Congreve earned the V.C. at Colenso in a brilliant dash to save the guns.

Thomas Wilson, Bishop of Sodor and Man, was born in a cottage in Burton, in 1663. The village school and master's house were built by him, and he framed rules for the well being of the free scholars. The master, before his little flock depart in the evening, must exhort them to say their prayers morning and evening, to be dutiful to their parents, and not to take God's name in vain. Bishop Wilson lies in Kirk Michael Churchyard. On his tombstone is this tribute: "This monument was erected by his son, Thomas Wilson, a native of this parish, who, in obedience to the express command of his father, declines giving him the character he justly deserves. Let this island speak the rest". The island does, and Cheshire too is proud of the man who "kept beggars from everybody's door but his own."

The fir-crowned rocky headland of Burton Point overlooks the broad marshes. Six feet of water washed the foot of the bluff at low water two hundred years ago, wearing away the sandstone foundations. In 1399 the Cheshire archers, the pick of Richard's army, embarked here for Ireland. Below the headland stretch miles and miles of saltings, tidal sand and slub, for until recent years high tides washed the embankment of the railway which crosses to the swingbridge at Connah's Quay. Far away, across the Dee Cut which creeps along the Welsh shore, black clouds of smoke rise from Deeside towns, veiling the heather-clad hills beyond; the steam from the racing Irish Mail, so far away, seems but to crawl below the foothills. Beside the railway are other embankments, battered and broken by fierce tides, which were built and rebuilt to reclaim the land. Natural causes and the Dee training wall have accomplished what they failed to do; save at high tides there is a great expanse of sheep-nibbled grassland, and the embankments now serve for refuges for the sheep when water drowns the saltings. Yonder a man is crossing the waste; he turns and twists, sometimes walking towards us, sometimes away; he is avoiding deep tidal gutters which intersect the marsh in every direction. Here, on the grass, dunlins feed in crowds, or paddle in the mud by the gutters, probing deep in the slub; here the yelping redshanks scream at the intruder, and the broad winged heron rises from the pool where he has been spearing dabs. There was once a heronry in Burton firs.

In winter, when bitter salt-laden wind sweeps over the flats, and hail and sleet sting like a whip-lash, the rocks of Burton are a welcome shelter; then; defying the storm, the wild geese fly over on strong pinion. What grand birds they are! Right in the teeth of the gale they come, yelping like a pack of hounds. Gabrial's hounds, superstitious folk call them, when they are heard at night.

> Oft have I heard my honoured mother say,
> How she has listened to Gabriel hounds—
> Those strange unearthly and mysterious sounds,
> Which on the ear through murkiest darkness fell;
> . . . .
> A spectral huntsman doomed to that long moonless chase.

Most of these geese are pink-footeds, though in former years bernacles resorted to the marshes in hundreds; at times other species come. The sporting colliers of Denhall, pothunters from Chester and elsewhere, and a few professional puntsmen, keep these birds on the move, giving them exercise, but seldom thin the skeins.

On the shore, below Burton Point, is a small white house where three generations of Kemps have farmed the marshes; huge flocks wander over the saltings, gathered when the tide threatens by intelligent dogs. Many years ago the inhabitants of Burton and Denhall were astonished by the strange behaviour of a new arrival, a man from Lincolnshire. William Kemp, nicknamed "Billy th' Duck," at all hours of the day and night put out his flat-bottomed punt and roused the echoes with his massive gun. Sometimes he would return with so many as thirty geese, which at half-a-crown apiece in Chester market was not bad work. His son learned wildfowling from him; on trackless wastes, in intricate gutters, he could find his way on the darkest night or thickest sea-fog; the "lums and gorings" or the "wild roads" were nothing to him. "Billy th' Duck" might kill thirty geese in a night, his son boasted thirty-five at a shot.

James Kemp loved to talk of the old sporting days. Somewhat bent with much stooping in the punt or crouching behind embankments when "flighting," tanned by wind and exposure, he was nevertheless a fine broad-shoulderd man; when he went for ducks or geese he meant to get them, and generally did. James kemp, last of the old school of wildfowlers, has gone. The upturned punt leans against the farm wall, the long muzzle-loading gun stands in a corner of the barn; the peaceful sheep browse on the short, hot grass, and the blue water, down below Parkgate, shimmers in the sun. There is little to suggest danger. But when white foam comes roaring o'er the level sands, when the wild nor'wester whips the spume from racing white-horses or rolls the sea-fog over the saltings, we realise what suggested Kingsley's verses:

"O Mary, go and call the cattle home,
And call the cattle home,
And call the cattle home,
Across the sands o' Dee:"
The western wind was wild and dank wi' foam,
And all alone went she.

The creeping tide came up along the sand,
And o'er and o'er the sand,
And round and round the sand,
As far as eye could see;
The blinding mist came down and hid the land—
And never home came she.

Denna Colleries were opened in 1750; at first coal was conveyed from the galleries, which burrowed nearly two miles under the tide, through underground canals, the boats forced slowly along by colliers lying on their backs and pushing with their feet on the roof. Now tramways are used. Between Denhall and Moorside stands the Old Quay House, where two hundred years ago thirty or forty feet of water filled the channel. The quay has gone, but the old ferry house, sometimes used as a prison, marks the spot where the Irish packet berthed. The river passage to Chester was impeded so far back as the days of Richard II; then Shotwick Quay was used. Silting continued until the sixteenth century, when the "New Kay" was constructed, and all went merrily until Parkgate was stranded and Liverpool and Holyhead had grown. At the Quay House Samuel Warren, it is said, wrote *Ten Thousand a Year.*

Neston, a market town of some importance, is full of quaint old houses and cottages. Miss Anna Seward, when on her way to Hoylake, wrote to a friend in 1794:—"with the odd anciety of Chester, we were much amused; it renders that city unique. Provokingly detained at Neston by waiting for horses, we were obliged to borrow the two dusky hours from seven to nine for travelling. They obliged us to take four, which being miserable Rosinantes, had difficulty enough in dragging us over roads of frightful ruggedness. If an infant Cynthia had not shed her pale gleams propitious, though faint, I know not what would have become of three cowards beneath the clouds of night and in roads so perilous.

"The clean and lonely village on the extreme verge of the peninsula is properly called Neston, originally, I suppose, Nest Town. It is indeed a nest from the storm of the ocean, which it immediately overhangs. We find pleasure in contemplating its neat little church and churchyard on that solitary eminence lashed by the tempestuous waves." Miss Seward's waves must have been tempestuous to have lashed the church of Neston!

Dugdale, in 1819 says:—"The inhabitants derive considerable advantage from the contiguity of Parkgate, which has of late years has become a convenient and fashionable bathing place. It is also celebrated as the station for some of the packets for Ireland, which generally sail to that country four times a week. The houses of Parkgate are chiefly disposed in one long range on the Dee banks, and are mostly neat modern buildings of brick. The inhabitants, who are rather numerous, derive their principal support from the expenditure of visitants who reside here in the bathing season." What were Llandudno, Colwyn, Rhyl, Blackpool, and Douglas like in 1819? Surely Parkgate should be a city now! A city! Look at poor old Parkgate to-day, and you will not talk of cities.

Less than a mile from Neston is Parkgate, the village "all on one side." Weston Point received its death-blow from the increase of commerce; lack of trade slew Parkgate. As I turn by Mr. Grenfell's school, once the old "George Hotel," and see the long line of decayed inns, hotels, and fashionable lodgings fronting the crubling esplanade, and look seaward at the miles and miles of sand and mud and far-distant shrimp boats lying over on their sides in Gayton Gut, I cry "Ichabod!" Where are the busy coaches? where the packets at the quay? where the bathing vans, and gaily dressed ladies? where is the quay itself? The hotels—converted into lodgings—look careworn and forlorn, while big-booted, jerseyed fishermen and barefooted, short-skirted women tramp the wet sands towards the boats which lie in the distant Gut.

Navigation of the Dee was difficult in the fourteenth century; in 1422 the commerce of Chester was lamentably decayed by reason of the "abundance of sands which had choked the creek," and in 1560 a collection was made in all churches of the kingdom to raise a fund to build the "New Kay" or New Haven. Then Parkgate was born. One hundred years later it was a prosperous port carrying nearly all the Irish traffic. Still the shifting sands caused inconvenience, and Yarranton says, "in the month of July, 1674, I was prevailed with by a person of honour to survey the River Dee running by the city of Chester to the Irish Sea, and finding the river choked with sand, that a vessel of 20 tons could not come to that noble city and the ships forced to lye at Neason in a very bad harbour, whereby the ships receive some damage, and trade is made so uncertain and changeable that the trade of Chester is much decayed and gone to Leverpoole." Improvements were made and Parkgate and Neston kept busy by the New Quay, till at the close of the eighteenth century Pennant tells that ships of 350 tons burden could reach the quays. There was abundance of water at Parkgate, and as summer holidays were becoming general, the village catered for a sea-bathing public. Coaches galore brought holiday-makers and passengers for Ireland; the hotels were full, and the lodging-house keepers reaped a harvest; Parkgate in fact, was one of the gayest towns in England. In 1754 Mrs Delaney wrote to a friend: "We have good reason to think we shall sail this evening—had we not come to Park Gate as we did, we should not have found room. People came every day, and the place is crowded."

Most of those who left any record of their passage to Ireland seem to have been impressed by the perils of the sea; John Wesley, however, having a calm sea, shut himself up in his travelling chaise and employed the time in reading the life of a notorious murderer. The crossing varied according to the wind, but thirteen or fourteen

PARKGATE

hours was good. Many boats were lost; in 1758, about seventy passengers of the *Dublin* were drowned; the crew of this boat consisted of a master, three sailers, and a boy! In an October gale in 1775 two boats floundered, and in 1806 the *King George* broke up on Hoyle Bank, only three or four being rescued out of 160 passengers. All the boats were not seaworthy, for Mrs Gamlin states that in 1897 an old Parkgate packet, built ninety years before, was still trading between Liverpool and Dublin. In addition to the Irish packets, sailing ferry boats crossed daily to Flint; these boats were often overcrowded, causing inconvenience and risk.

The beautiful Lady Hamilton, then Mrs Hart, visited Parkgate in 1784 to remove some disfiguring eruption by the application of salt water. "You can't think," she says, "how soult the water is, and there is a many laidys bathing here." She was troubled by the expense of the bathing horse and the cost of her dress, which amounted to 1s. 2d. per day. "It is a great expense, and it fretts me wen I think of it." Handel was another visitor when on his way to Ireland; it is said that he composed the "Messiah" at the "George Hotel" while waiting for his boat, though Mrs Gamlin's statement that the oratorio was performed for the first time in Dublin may be the explanation. Mrs Fitzherbert was another summer visitor, renting a house on the front; and the London papers of the time gave long lists of "sea dippers" at this fashionable seaside resort.

The training wall for the New Cut gave the death-blow to Parkgate; currents were altered, the steep bank up which labouring horses dragged the bathing machines disappeared, and a great waste of sand silted up the approach to the esplanade; soon the pier was buried beneath the invading sand. And what is Parkgate now? The "George" is a boys school; the theatre, where fashionable visitors went to see Liston, the elder Mathews, Miss O'Neil and Miss Foote, a schoolroom; the Assembly Rooms may still be picked out by their elaborate but ancient balcony railings; the sea wall which kept back the tide has little to do but restrain the encroachment of sand. Yet Parkgate is reviving; gables which a few years ago were in ruins are now repaired, breaches in the seawall have been mended, and the place generally restored. Many years ago, even before its days of prosperity, Parkgate was a place for the herring fishery; that schoolroom, once a theatre, was in earlier times a curing house. Even in Pennant's days herrings were dropping their annual visits to the Dee, and those which were caught were "shotton and meagre"; but the Chester hawkers, a few years ago, if their fish were fine, cried them as "Parkgate herrings."

The tide is out. Across the waste of wet sand and mud comes the wail of Curlew, almost the only sign of life. In the far distance a twinkling line of foam is crawling onwards; the fisher-folk at Gayton are manning their boats; the carts which have taken down the nets are returning to the shore. The beacon bouy in the Deep swings round; Bug Swash swells till Big Ben is covered; and far-off Caldy Blacks sink beneath the waves. The tide is coming. Parkgate Deep is full, and the boats at Heswall and Gayton strain on their anchors; guts are now broad rivers and bank after bank is lost beneath the racing waters, for the sea comes in apace across the flats. Then the flood swings up, kissing the forsaken wall, and almost at once all is over; the water is racing back to the ocean bearing on its ebb the shrimpers of Parkgate.

This then, is what kept Parkgate alive. Shrimping and trawling, the fisher-folk make a fair living, and when the salmon are running up they catch good fish along the Parkgate shore, for some salmon cling to the old channel and avoid the New Cut.

The tide has come and gone so quickly that we can scarce realise that for a short period there was a stretch of water from the sea-wall to the far-off shores of Wales; harder still to believe that almost within memory a schooner was driven on a high tide up one of the narrow streets.

In the open space at the far end of the village cattle were penned after they had swum ashore from the Irish boats; down these narrow passages the sea-folk lived, augmenting their incomes by smuggling and, it is hinted, by the worse crime of wrecking. Smugglers and wreckers, fashionable bathers and cross-channel travellers have gone for ever; but there is hope for the place yet. The air is as good as it ever was, the western breezes healthy and salt-laden, the distant hills of Wales are beautiful as of yore; improved railway facilities are turning Desside villages into residential outskirts of Liverpool, and in time Greater Liverpool will reach Parkgate. A century ago a ship canal to Manchester was suggested with Parkgate as the seaward end. Liverpool scoffed.

> These lords of the shuttle,
>   By a process most subtle,
> A canal mean to cut from the ocean,
>   And the great Irish Sea
>   They'll unite with the Dee.
> But it's a Fiddle de Dee I've a notion.

This was one of the many skits in Liverpool papers. The Dee scheme fell through but Manchester has got its way. Parkgate will not be a Western Point or an Eastham, but is already a more desirable place. The tumble-down houses have been rebuilt, many new ones erected on its outskirts; the toilers from overcrowded Liverpool have rescued Parkgate.

At the end of the promenade the road turns by the old Ferry House and passes the gates of Leighton Hall—the Park Gates—and a little further on the West Kirby road is reached. Gayton, the next Deeside village, is growing fast. William of Orange stayed at Gayton Hall when on his way to the Battle of the Boyne, and knighted his host, Sir William Clegg. The columbarium in the grounds was built in 1663.

Between the river and the heather clothed Beacon Hill is Heswall, now a mainly residential village, and a tablet on the boundary wall of one house marks the site of the Hassle Walle; the church contains some ancient fonts, carved stones, and memorials of past Heswall worthies. On the heather-clad Heswall Hill, where sandstone crops out here and there, the air is pure and the view delightful; the summits of Heswall Hill and Caldy Hill beyond were called the Beacons. Warning fires, no doubt, burnt here when Danish ships—black pirate craft with strange carved dragons on their prows—crept up the Dee towards Chester. When, "like volcanoes, flared to heaven the stormy hills of Wales," Heswall and Caldy fires would pass the message to Halton and Lancaster; a few years later instructions were sent to keep the fires ready and appoint reliable watchers. In pre-lighthouse days these beacons were guides for the Dee shipping, and a windmill on Caldy Hill was a mariner's mark; it was wrecked in a storm and a permanent landmark erected in 1841.

Thurstaston Hall is close beside the modern church with the ivy-covered tower of the older church standing detached in the churchyard. The Hall has portions which were built five hundred years ago, and others added two centuries later; the east wing is modern. A ghost, a little old lady who pulls a bell-rope, kindly haunted an artist who was staying in the house, and he sketched her while she stood beside his bed.

Irby Hall, once a grange of the monks of St Werburgh, moated and fortified, stands a little to the right. The present Hall, with a restored black and white front, has good seventeenth-century work at the back, but the moat is perhaps all that remains of the grange. Irby is still a quaint, old fashioned village.

Thurstaston is perched high on breezy hills overlooking the Dee, but where is the Port of Dawpool? An old Wirral hunting song tells of a wonderful hare that was started near the Point of Ayre, ran through Talacre and Mostyn, crossed the river and finally returned via Chester to Wales, where it ended its days. On the Welsh shore we learn—

> Yett ye hare had care of her feete
> For fere of falling in an ould cole pitte,

but nevertheless Puss found coal-mining convenient, for she crossed to Dawpool in a coal-boat. The only other passenger of note that I find recorded as landing at Dawpool was Dean Swift; he disembarked here in 1707 and rode to Parkgate. "Dorpoll," or "Darpool," was one of the ports whence boats for Ireland sailed. In 1822 Telford, the great engineer, was building the Port of Dawpool; in the *Gentleman's Magazine* for that year, we learn that—"Independently of the general accommodation which packets would afford at that station, the ready communication between Dublin and the depot at Chester, where nearly 40,000 stand of arms are kept, and the warlike stores, is of vital importance, especially at a time when the sister island is in a state of dangerous fermentation." The point of embarkation was getting further and further from Chester, but Liverpool was then making rapid strides, and the port, if ever finished, was abandoned; no trace remains.

A large detached rock or boulder on Thurstaston Common, now a lung for Liverpool, has caused speculation; the stone of Thor, "Thors-stane-ton," was Picton believes, erected by the Danes in memory of the battle of Brunnenburgh. Would the Danes put up a stone to commemorate defeat? Possibly it is Druidical, or left when vast geological upheavals moulded the hills of Wirral.

The villas of West Kirby cluster on the lower slopes of Grange or Beacon Hill. This seaside resort yearly gains popularity; not only do many visit West Kirby in summer, but doctors send weaklings to breath the health-giving breezes and recruit. West Kirby boasts a tradition, which has good foundation, the possession of one of the earliest Christian churches in England, for the church, dedicated to St Bridget, may stand where Irish missionaries landed and set up the Cross.

West Kirby and Hoylake are now continuous. When Nixon was asked what place would be a sanctuary in evil days, he replied, "God's Croft, between Mersey and Dee"; this western extremity of Wirral is "God's Croft." The golfer has annexed these sand-hills, a good thing for Hoylake but not so good for the local fauna and flora; yet the maram clothed dunes and the marshy spots between are beautiful with many coast-loving plants—creeping roses, pale blue-grey sea-holly, thrift, and yellow sea-poppy. Many of these levels, where water lay, are now "greens"; the cry of "fore" and warning notices damp the ardour of the naturalist. Still the natter-jack ambles across the flats, the lizard suns itself in the star-grass, the blue butterfly clings head-downwards on the rushes when the sun is clouded over, and in March the rare moth, Nyssia zonaria, hunts for its wingless spouse amongst the sand-hill plants.

Shops with glass-covered colonnades, smooth asphalted roads where blown sand lies in ridges—delightfully clean dirt—a long ever-growing promenade, rows of neat lodging houses and tree-lined streets are Hoylake to-day. How different from the scattered, sand-buried village, smelling of shrimps, where the cocklers lived on the shore of Hyle Lake. The great East Hoyle Bank lies seaward, a natural breakwater, leaving the narrow channel, the lake, a quiet harbour. Two hundred years ago this lake, then half a mile wide, was many feet deep close to the sea front, and crowds of large craft would shelter here till tide or wind was favourable; now at low water one may, like the cockle-hunters, wade the channel and walk upon the bank—but beware of the tide! Liverpool tugs pick up sail-ing craft far away on the Welsh coast, and the shallow channel now shelters a few fishing boats. Hoylake has grown, but its old industry is not dead. Women and men still rake for fluted cockles on the banks. "The biggest scrat in all Hoylake," an old term of reproach, had origin in cockle rakes.

Miss Seward, writing in 1794, says, "The glassy smoothness of this marine lake affords charming bathing for cowards." "High Lake," she continues, "is a new place. The house built by Sir John Stanley was finished only in 1792. The apartments are handsome and commodious, and the accommodation wonderfully comfortable for a situation without either town, or even village, in its neighbourhood." This, the "Royal Hotel," then stood almost alone amongst sandhills. From Hoylake we may follow the example of pilgrims to Lindisfarne.

> Dryshod o'er sands twice every day,
> The pilgrims to the shrine find way;
> Twice every day the waves efface
> Of staves and sandal'd feet the trace.

"In the utmost brink of this Promontory," says Camden, "lieth a small hungry barren and sandy isle, called Il-bre." Just a mile from the weathered red rocks of Hilbre Point rise the three islets of Hilbre, sandstone bluffs covered with short, salt-encrusted turf, which it is possible at low tide to reach from West Kirby or by the wetter crossing from Hoylake. Skirting the deepest pools and gutters I arrive at the "Lacus de Hilburgheye," or the "Heye-pol," and land on the island "where Deva weds the sea." Leyland was right," the ground is sandy and hath conies"; for rabbits prick up their pink ears and dive out of sight into their burrows, and wheatears chack and flirt their tails amongst the thrift. There was a "Capella de Hilburgheye" so far back as 1081, but no trace remains of church or monastic cell, and no "sort of superstitious fools," as Holinshead calls them, now "cherish and maintain" the monks of St Hilburgh, although many years ago a devotional cross was discovered buried in sand on part of the island.

Richard, Earl of Chester, who was drowned in the White Ship, got into trouble with fiery Welshmen when on pilgrimage to the shrine of St. Winifred; he shut himself up in Basingwerke Abbey, and by some means acquainted his constable, the Baron of Halton, that he was in sore distress. Fitz Nigel, whose knowledge of geography was faulty, hurried to Hilbre, where, of course, he was stopped by the sea; a monk, however, told him to offer supplication to St. Werburgh, who smiled upon him and divided the waters so that he could cross to succour his lord. The great bank that surrounds Hilbre is Constable Sands, in memory of the event, or of the monastic legend.

A cave on the seaward side of the island, said to have been excavated by a monk, is the scene of Edgerton Legh's ballad, "The Lady's Shelf."

> There is a cave with pink flowers dight
> (Bairns "Lady Cushions" call);
> Hence you may gaze on Ocean's might
> Far grandest scene of all.

One day the monk, when visiting his cell, discovered the body of a maiden left by the tide. He bore her to safety and she recovered sufficiently to tell her sad story; she was the Lord of Shotwick's daughter, and her lover, Edgar, had saved her from many perils, but her father refused to recognise him as a suitor, and betrothed her to a Welsh knight she did not favour. On her way to her new home, having been told that Edgar was dead, she jumped or tumbled overboard, when the boat was rounding the Point of Ayr, and her bereaved sire, when too late, called out that Edgar was alive and she might have him if only she would come back. Then she died.

Sir Edward Stanley, reporting on the fortifications of Cheshire during the Armada scare, declared Hilbre to be "a place very parlus if the enemy should possess it ever. The soldier would stop our passage into Ireland." Spain, had she captured Hilbre, might have made it her Rock of Gibralter!

Hilbre Island has interest for the naturalist. Migratory birds stop to rest on passage, wild geese and swans—true wild swans, whoopers and Bewick's—rare divers and grebes, seals and whales, all have been noted. One day a young hedgehog turned up. Had it wandered across the sands? Had it swum ashore from some passing boat? Or had St. Werburgh kindly divided the waters for it to cross dryshod from Wales? Now it happened that three lively yachtsmen were visiting the resident's officer when this urchin was discovered; to their delight Mr Jones held forth on the strange occurrences with great gravity, until it dawned upon them that he was remarking the curious habit of the hedgehog of taking passage on a yacht.

When "Hyle Lake" was a refuge for Liverpool shipping the sailors used to pull to the island, for in those days a disreputable public-house was kept by a couple whose character we learn from Richard Ayton, who visited Hilbre in 1813. They gained their living in other ways than selling drink; there was plenty of smuggling, and a bit of wrecking might be lucrative, besides the pickings from any drowned body washed ashore; at any rate, the man and his wife, who was just as keen in illicit longshore pursuits as her husband, and like him wore trousers, amassed a considerable fortune.

But the tide is swelling in Hilbre Swash; it is time to paddle back towards the Cheshire shore. It is unwise to stay too long on Hilbre.

CHAPTER 2
NORTHERN AND EASTERN WIRRAL

THE coast from Hilbre Point to New Brighton was once lined with sand-hills which protected the low-lying marshes of North Wirral from encroachment by the sea. Now, these sand-hills are built upon or rented by golfers; between Leasowe and Meols the embankment renders them unnecessary, and here has sprung with mushroom growth the strange Caravan town of Moreton. Near Dove Point, no connection with the stock-doves which bred in the rabbit burrows, but a corruption of "dhuv" or black, a large tract of buried forest is exposed. Submerged for-est-lands, which crop up along this and the Lancashire coast, lie between the sand-hills and the sea; black turfy soil studded with stocks and roots of trees, while ancient timbers lie prone half buried in the earth. Some of these are of considerable size; they are oak, birch, and conifers, but the largest, black with age and waterlogged, have been broken up or removed. Webb speaks of fir-trees buried in the mosses—"some are of opinion that they have lain there ever since Noah's flood," and tells how they are dug up for firewood or to make candle-lights, but he does not speak specially of the buried forests of Wirral. The sea, eating into this mossland, reveals the changes which the coast has undergone; shifting sand covered the forest, trees rotted and fell, and dunes rose high above their stumps. Then the sand was washed or blown away, and once more the wave laid bare the woodlands; from the deep inlets where storms have torn away great masses of peat, it will not be long before all traces of the forests have disappeared.

In these forests many strange things have been found; bones and teeth of long extinct animals, boars, deer and cattle, horn-cores of great wild *Bos primigenius* and the smaller domesticated *Bos longifrons*. Roman and medieval coins, instruments, articles of apparel such as buckles, pins and clasps, metal implements of all sorts and a few spears, knives, and warlike tools, have also been revealed. But more recent treasure sometimes turns up; one morning Mrs Gamlin tells, Sir Edward Cust came down to breakfast at Leasowe Castle and found no servant to wait upon him. At last a kitchen maid turned up and stammered out: "Please, Sir Edward, they're all on the shore picking up goulden guineas." There they were, butler, cook and housemaid, stable-boy and groom, gathering a store of coins which a low tide had exposed. These guineas were supposed to have been lost with one of the ships which carried soldiers of the Prince of Orange to Ireland.

Bidston Hill, inland from Great Meols, commands a far-reaching prospect of Wallasey flats and the sandbanks of Liverpool Bay. The old lighthouse and observatory crown the summit, and modern houses peep out amongst the trees which clothe the slopes; Bidston is perhaps the healthiest and best situated residential district round Liverpool. Telford, standing on the summit and looking east, declared that Liverpool was on the wrong side of the Mersey. The Hill, with its furze, heather, and rocks, is preserved as an open space by Birkenhead.

The village of Bidston clusters round its old church at the foot of the hill. "It was a little grey village—so very grey indeed, and venerable and quaint, that no flaunting red brick had dared to show itself and break the uniform tint of its gabled antiquity," when Christopher Tadpole visited the "Ring o' Bells" "And the old Grange with its mullioned windows and its ivy-covered gateway was the greyest of all."

Bidston is grey to-day, but the red brick and modern half-timber have dared to invade it, and the "Ring o' Bell" is gone. A labourer whom I questioned about the old inn which caught Albert Smith's fancy, only knew the "Ham and Eggs." But the Grange is there, grey as ever, in spite of alterations made in the early part of the last century. Bidston Hall, which Smith calls the Grange, is irregular and quaint; its gateway, "greyest of all," is decorated with three strange ornaments which long were believed to represent two decanters and a punchbowl. This "punchbowl" had been lost, but has been restored from an old drawing, upsetting the tradition, for it is a similar ornament to the other two. Are these the "ham and eggs," for no inn has this title?

BIDSTON HALL

Round the Deer Park—deer park on longer—ran a great wall, very high and four feet thick at the base, built, it is supposed, by Royal grant in or about 1408. Fragments remain, known locally as "The Penny-a-day Dyke," the pay of the workmen who raised it, according to local tradition. An Earl of Derby built the present Hall when James I was king, but it was not long a family possession. The heroic widow who defended Lathom House, when her estates were ruined by Parliamentary wars, sold Bidston to a London lawyer, who parted with it to the extravagant Lord Kingston. Sir Robert Vyner, banker and pawnbroker to needy monarchs, foreclosed a mortgage and took the property. Vyner designed our copper coinage, giving to Britannia the likeness of Miss Frances Stewart, one of the many favourites of his client, Charles II.

The story that the Bidston property was played for, lost and won on the ace of clubs is fiction. On the site once stood a summer house, built in the shape of the ace, and here the conspirators of the Rye House Plot met. Monmouth had come to Chester ostensibly to attend Wallasey races, and Sir Peter Shakerley reported all that transpired to the Court. The Duke rode his own horse and won the £60 plate, which he forthwith presented to his goddaughter, the Mayor of Chester's child; afterward he raced on foot, both with and without boots, with a Cambridge man named Cutts, again winning in both cases. Bonfires were lighted in Chester to celebrate his victory, for the Duke was popular, but riots resulted from differences in party opinion. Monmouth no doubt was pleased when a child was brought to him to be touched for the king's evil.

Wallasey was a favourite sporting centre long before this time; Web tells of the "fair sands, or plains, upon the shore of the sea, which, for the fitness for such a purpose, allure the gentlemen and others" ("others" went to race meetings even then) "oft to appoint great matches and ventre no small sums in trying the swiftness of their horses." Leasowe Castle was originally a racing box, built by the fifth Earl of Derby somewhere about 1593; it has since been called the New Hall and Mockbeggar Hall, and served many purposes. There is a mystery about this Earl; he was nearest kinsman, save for Queen Elizabeth, to Henry VIII, and conspirators suggested a possible rising. Lord Derby, loyal to the backbone, refused, and shortly afterwards died suddenly. It was whispered that these rebels knew why. The Manor passed to the Egertons of Oulton, and during the Civil War fell into ruins; then it was said that it earned the name of Mockbeggar Hall. In Collins' *Pilot*, published in 1690, Mockbeggar Wharf, the name still given to the foreshore, first appears. Sir Edward Cust added to its structure; one room he panelled with woodwork from the Star Chamber of Westminster, and another with bog-oak from Leasowe shore.

Wallasey Marshes lie behind the Embankment—a fine engineering work and a pleasant promenade. Perhaps at some remote period this flat land was the mouth of the Mersey, the shore to the north continuous with the Lancashire coast. The ditches and inland pools on the low-lying fields are full of a yellow button-like flower which has puzzled many botanists, for it is not native in our islands. *Cotula coronopifolia*, at one time cultivated in the gardens of the Castle, has established itself in the country without, and spread and multiplied; an interesting addition to the flora. Prawns abound in many of the pools, even where water is fresh; they too benefit by a change of surroundings, though now cut off from the sea. This part of Wirral is the County Council sanctuary for birds; in autumn the fields are resorted to by immense numbers of small waders when the mudflats and banks are covered by the tide; the wheeling, flashing flocks of dunlins and ringed plovers give life and beauty to the flats.

Near the Docks Station I cross the end of Wallasey Pool, leaving Wallasey on my left, and ride through Liscard to New Brighton. The old tower of Wallasey Church, which was built in 1530, stands a little distant from the modern building; it was all that was saved from the fire in 1857. A record of Wallasey Church states that "the auntient cottagers have order in seates according to the worthiness of there landlordes"; what is the meaning of worthy?

New Brighton is a lesser Blackpool, with a promenade pier and, until recently, a lofty tower. The fort which stands beside the lighthouse on a red rock is more picturesque than effective; the Mersey defences are not impregnable, but a hostile fleet would be in diffi-culties were the bouys removed from the intricate channels of Liv-erpool Bay. As a watering place New Brighton is not a success; Lancashire trippers who bathe here walk far to get knee-deep. Donkey and horse-riding is an amusement, especially to spectators, and there is the pier. The promenade was formerly know as "Ham and Egg Terrace," where coy maidens lured pleasure seekers to enter gaudy saloons, where oysters, shrimps, aerated waters, and other luxuries could be obtained, but the stock dish—the *bonne bouche*—was ham and eggs. To-day the Terrace supplies all the entertainments and other charms of the tripper's seaside resort.

The three-mile ride to Birkenhead is urban, almost metropolitan when the Great Float is passed. Woodside Stage, the most impor-tant of the Cheshire ferries, is a busy scene; the Mersey tunnel does not lessen the bustle. Skilfully handled, crowded ferry-boats hurry backwards and forwards across the river, dodging each other and the shipping. Watch them come rushing towards the stage as if they wished to sink it, and see how in spite of a strong tide they swing up alongside without a bump; with screws fore and aft, they are more in the hands of the captain and engineer than the steers-man. The "thousand masts" of Mersey are a strange contrast to the forsaken Dee; Birkenhead and Liverpool are the hub of one of the world's commercial wheels.

Little over a hundred years ago there were only sixteen houses in Birkenhead, but by the middle of the last century, when the Great Float, the largest of the docks, was completed, there were over two thousand, and the town was rapidly growing. It has been called, not without reason, "Liverpool's Bedroom."

Shipbuilding is the industry of Birkenhead; from Laird's yard, in 1829, emerged the first iron boat built in England. In the sixties, when a bitter cry for cotton came from every town in Lancashire, Liverpool and Birkenhead merchants made rapid but risky fortunes by blockade-running. Then it was that a boat steamed out of Laird's yard, normally to run the blockade; England narrowly escaped war with America owing to the damage done by this pseudo-blockade runner, really privateer, the *Alabama*.

The remains of the Benedictine monastery of Birkenhead stand between the busy streets and busier river hard by the Monk's Ferry. Somewhere about 1150 Hamo de Masci of Dunham founded the Priory, which for many years was used as an hostelry, where travellers detained by stress of weather could stay till the monks ferried them across to Liverpool. A mythical story tells that when the monastic houses were dissolved the monks fled with treasure down an underground passage, but a portion of the roof falling in, they and the treasure were buried for ever.

BIRKENHEAD PRIORY—THE CHAPTER HOUSE

The monastic house by the Priory became Birkenhead Hall, and in the seventeenth century belonged to the Powell family; when it was decided to purchase the ruins of the Abbey for the Corporation, a descendant of the family headed the subscription list. The Hall has gone; what has become of its ghost? Sir Thomas Powell, last of that name to own the Priory, offended his wife by paying attention to her maid; so my lady, while her maid was dressing her, pushed the damsel over the banisters and fled to a foreign convent. Sir Thomas buried the murdered girl at his estate in Wales, and died a lonely, embittered man; but the maid's spirit returned to the staircase and haunted the scene of the tragedy.

"The village of Oxton," says Ormerod, "is mean and small, composed of wretched straggling huts, amongst roads only not impassable. The township occupies an eminence which commands a full view of the buildings and shipping of Liverpool, exhibiting a picture resembling metropolitan bustle and splendour, almost immediately below the eye; but no degree of civilisation or improvement has reached this part of the opposite shore, which is a scene of solitude, broken in upon only by the voice of the cowherd or the cry of the plover. Bleak and barren moors stretch round it in every direction, and exhibit an unmixed scene of poverty and desolation." And now! The higher we rise the more we leave the town behind and the more the residential the district becomes, till Birkenhead, the river, and Liverpool are mapped below. In the "Sloyne," Atlantic greyhounds rest at anchor, and a Liverpool man will point out each by its build or funnel. Tranmere, home of the four Randle Holmes, is at the foot of the hill. The first Randle cared so little about honours that he paid a fine of £10 rather than be knighted at the coronation of Charles I, yet he served his country as Sheriff and Mayor of Chester. The third Holme wrote *The Academie of Armory*, which he wisely says "is to be understood by few"; it contains all sorts of matter, including "the proper mode of blazoning God the Father, the Son, and the Holy Spirit, cherubim and seraphim. Heathen gods and goddesses, demigods and country gods, holy orders of angels, and the infernal order of devils, and all live animals in which there is either life or motion." It gives a coat of arms for almost every subject under the sun, comprising such diverse things as cock-fighting, punishment in hell, palmistry, grammar, billiards and dreams. The manuscripts, however, collected by these four Cheshire men, and their investigation of ancient monuments, are of the greatest value.

Higher up the river is Rock Ferry, here Nathaniel Hawthorne lived when came to Liverpool, and beyond again is New Ferry. Part of this ferry collapsed during a heavy gale, and some time later a mass of timber was found floating in the Irish Sea, bearing the admonition that "No vessels must anchor here." A mile or two inland from Oxton is Woodchurch, its church tower strengthened by massive buttresses.

The road that leads south along the ridge from Oxton leads to Storeton, where amongst the fir-woods are famous quarries for building stone, renowned amongst geologists for the frequent traces revealed upon the flags of former Wirral inhabitants. That great creature, Labyrinthodon, hoped about the ancient beaches which hardened into Keuper sandstones, and in the soft tidal sand left its footmarks, and the casts rather than the indentations of the perambulations are found, along with ripple marks, when the stones are split. Examples of these hand-like marks may be seen in many museums, and in out-of-the-way places, as in an entry to Bowdon, weathered flags bearing these footprints in the sands of time have taught many an early lesson in geology.

The deep gorges, the furze and bramble-grown excavations, and the worn deserted rails show the antiquity of Storeton quarries; not that they are deserted, for excellent stone is still obtained; but in places far remote from the present quarries there are huge excavations, long unworked. Storeton Hall lies a little to the right, on a hill apart from the quarried ridge. Many traces remain of the pack-tracks and roughly paved lanes which radiated from the home of the Sylvesters, foresters of Wirral. Then came the Stanleys from Stoneleigh and settled in the district, and at the close of the fourteenth century William de Stanley built Storeton Hall; the Cheshire Stanleys are descended from the Storeton settlers. Only a fragment of Sir William's house remains, now screened by a new barn. Attached to the farm buildings of the present Hall is a high wall containing an ancient doorway and a large pointed window. Looking at it from the farmyard we see only the inside of one of the great hall windows, for the cowshed beyond is built against the exterior of the old house.

Storeton has its story of an elopement as romantic as that of Haddon or the legend of Lochinvar; through this clandestine marriage the Stanleys obtained the master-forestership of Wirral and its estates and revenues. John de Stanley, over six hundred years ago, was entertaining Sir Philip de Bamville and his family. Joan, Sir

WOODCHURCH

Philip's eighteen-year-old daughter, had no liking for the marriage that her father had arranged for her with his stepson, so while festivities were at their height she quietly slipped away. Young William Stanley was waiting with saddled steeds; into the saddle she sprang, and away down the rough Wirral tracks, over the Gowy marshes, across the great Cheshire plain, the two young lovers spurred to Astbury. In that ancient church, William declared—we have the actual words sworn to by trustworthy witnesses—"Joan, I plight thee my troth to take and hold thee as my lawful wife unto my life's

STORETON HALL

end," and the happy girl replied, "I, Joan take thee, William, as my lawful husband." No doubt the knight was wroth; no doubt he blamed John Stanley and his heady beer for hoodwinking him, but the marriage was legal, and the Stanleys were powerful, so all ended well.

Not far from Storeton, in the centre of Wirral, is Brimstage, or Brunstath, where at the Hall exists a portion of an ancient building, perhaps a peel tower. Sir Hugh de Hulse built this tower—a portion of his castle—in 1398; it is a strong keep or peel, the vaulted lower story of which was the chapel.

One monument in the church at Higher Bebington is older than most church decorations, for in the porch, above the door, is a triangular stone from the quarries hard by, adorned with three or four footmarks of the amphibious Labyrinthodon. Lower Bebington Church is more interesting. Hawthorne was much struck by this old church. "The steeple has ivy on it," he says, "and looks old, old, old; so does the whole church, though portions of it have been renewed, but not so as to impair the appearance of heavy substantial endurance, and long, long decay, which may go on hundreds of years longer before the church is a ruin. . . . . Close to the wall of the church, beside the door, there was an ancient baptismal font of stone. In fact, it was a pile of roughly-hewn stone steps, five or six feet high, with a block of stone at the summit, in which was a hollow about as big as a wash-bowl. It was full of rain water." So it is now; but is it a font or the remains of a village cross? Some pillars in the south aisle are late Norman, excellently preserved; the others late Perpendicular. In the choir-stalls are quaint misereres; one, a pelican feeding its young, is both interesting and amusing. Five shillings a year was the rent of a cow in Bebington, for under a useful benefaction the poor parishioners were supplied with a cow at this moderate charge; it was, however, stipulated that the animal should be returned at the end of the year in good repair.

Leaving the church, with its "old, old, old" broached spire, I see across the railway some red-tiled, magpie buildings. How often we find rural beauties destroyed by commerce, land bare and barren, sky dulled by smoke; worse still when we come across dirty herded streets where insanitary cottages are thrown together anyhow for the dwellings of "hands." The soap trade is often responsible for accumulation of dirt, and most unpleasant odours. Is filth and squalor necessary? Look at yonder village, clean and neat; look at those roads lined with young elms and chestnuts, at the half-timbered cottages each with its garden plot, at the stone bridge, the little church, the fine halls and immense works. This is indeed a soap-works and its village. Not many years ago between the Bebington road and the river all was grazing land or swamp—mostly the latter, when Lever Brothers chose the spot for the manufactory of Sunlight Soap. In building they considered the welfare of those they

BRIMSTAGE HALL

employed; they built Port Sunlight with generous hand, erecting some six hundred sanitary and tasteful houses for their three thousand odd employees; they gave them a temperance inn, and dining halls, the first of which Gladstone opened in 1891. Port Sunlight is a lasting honour to the late Lord Leverhulme and his helpers.

St. Patrick sailed up the Mersey and landed in the little creek now called Bromborough Pool, baptizing at the well which retains his name, a well famous for its petrifying properties. Bromborough, the next village, claims to be the site of the battle of Brunanburgh, when, in 937, Æethelstan and Edmund Æetheling, with their West Saxons and Mercian troops, defeated invading Danes, who had landed 30,000 soldiers, Danes, Norwegians, Irish and Scotch. The point of landing of the 615 ships, and the site of the battle, are matters of dispute; some place the battle on the Humber. But a battle was fought about this time in Wirral, and Bromborough is as likely a spot as any.

The Court House, by the side of Bromborough Pool, was built by the Hardwares towards the end of the seventeenth century. The family were supporters of Nonconformity—Mathew Henry married a daughter of the house—and Harrison, the ejected Puritan divine, preached at the court when he left Chester. The Hall, another old house, was built by Bishop Bridgman, we learn from an article in the *Gentleman's Magazine* for 1762. In the same article is a quaint description of the petrifying well and of a creature of zoological interest. "A kind of reptile, called by the inhabitants 'long worms,' is very common here in the sandy lanes and hedges, and a poor girl, who lived here, once fed one of them, which became so tame as to creep round her arm and receive its food from her without injuring her." The blindworm is not extinct in Wirral; if this is the creature meant, how could it injure her?

At Eastham Ferry, the Manchester Ship Canal enters the tidal Mersey, after winding round the southern shore of the river, thus avoiding difficult channels and shifting sandbanks. Eastham Church has an octagonal broach spire nearly as ancient as Bebington; Hawthorne said that Eastham was "the finest old English village" that he had come across. The old yew in the churchyard looks sickly; like so many churchyard yews, its days are numbered; according to local report, it is over a thousand years old!

The road to the left leads towards Hooton, the great house built in 1778, for the Earls of Derby, and used, until recently, as a centre for racing, polo, golf, and other sports in the park, which covers some three hundred acres. Now, Liverpool demands it for residential extension.

Staunch Catholics were the Stanleys of Hooton, yet when Spain was threatening, Rowland Stanley was amongst the largest subscribers to the defence fund. His son Sir William was a soldier of fortune, who won honours by his victory over the Irish rebels in Munster, when his gallant band held superior numbers at bay for eight hours. When governor of Deventer under Leicester, he treated the burgomasters with scant civility. "Now fetch me the keys of the gate and deliver me them straight, and you shall all die," he commanded the trembling city fathers. Babington's conspiracy to place Mary Queen of Scots on the throne found favour in his sight; he urged his lawless troops to take service under the flag of Spain, and sank so low as to point out vulnerable spots for the attacks of the Armada. The Hooton family is no more. Sir William Massey Stanley ruined the estates by extravagance. When he sold his property to pay his debts, Napoleon III, who had been his guest, helped him to meet his creditors.

A lane running towards the river is the way to Poole. There were Pooles by the Mersey when Edward I was king, and the Pooles lived here until a few years ago. Probably Sir William Poole, Sheriff of Chester under Henry VIII built part of the present Hall; there is, however, a stone in the garden which stood above one of the fireplaces, now hidden beneath rockery plants, bearing the date 1570 and the initials I.P and K.P. Poole is perhaps the finest of the old Wirral halls; a tall octagonal turret stands at either end of the east front, and a great embattled porch rises above the front doorway. The stone portions, old though they are, are young compared with the overhanging timbered gable at the back; probably at one time the whole was timbered. Within are panelled rooms and a closed underground passage, which tradition affirms was connected with the similar passage at Stanlow Point, a long subterranean walk for the monks of Stanlow or devout Catholics of Poole.

The old clock on the front does not mark time now; its massive weights decorate the rockery. These weights formerly dropped down

POOLE HALL

an enclosed wooden shaft outside the walls. Very grey and weathered are the ancient walls of Poole, rather uncertain the perpendiculars of those strange turrets. The place has seen many years, and many vicissitudes, for the Pooles, like the Stanleys, suffered persecution for their faith.

A great mound stands as a background to Poole—Mount Manisty, said to be the largest hill raised by human hands, is a spoil-bank from the Ship Canal. Close to this point the canal is 120 feet wide, and the embankment that separates it from the river 140 feet across its base and half that width at the top. There is now a road direct from Poole to Ellesmere Port, the busy town which surrounds the docks at the end of that Cheshire canal, the Shropshire Union. Fifty coasters and fifty flats can load and unload in the Ship Canal opposite the great grain elevator, as prominent an object as Mount Manisty. Ellesmere Port is interesting, but not beautiful; I pass on to Whitby, where about a mile form the road is the site of one of the granges of Stanlow; the terraced moat of Grange Cow Worth can still be seen, but the ruins and pavement which the plough revealed have been removed.

Little Stanney, just beyond Whitby, was the home of the Bunburys; they lived in the moated Hall and the house at the far end of the street, called Rake Hall. It is said that uproarious convivial meetings gave the place its name, but as there is a Rake Hall in Bromborough and a Rake Lane in Eastham, there may be another meaning.

It is not far to Chester through Stoke and Upton. On the way I pass Wervin, where an ancient chapel was converted or perverted into a cowshed. Butter Hill, which is hardly an eminence and lies on the right, was supposed to have been named during a Chester plague. The Wirral farmers brought their provisions here and left them for the plague-infected inhabitants. I re-enter Chester by Northgate.

THE MANCHESTER SHIP CANAL